GAME BASI

TO PREVENT INFECTION

FROM COVID-19

PETER CHEW

PCET VENTURES (003368687-P)

Email:peterchew999@hotmail.my

ISBN: 978-1-387-74537-1

© Peter Chew 2022

Cover Design : Peter Chew

Cover Image: Freepik Premium

 Author: Peter Chew

Peter Chew is Biochemist., Mathematician, Inventor and Global issue analyst, Reviewer for Europe Publisher (Eliva Press) , Engineering Mathematics Lecturer , Medical device Consultant of The Best Perfect Sdn. Bhd and President of Research and Development Secondary School (IND) for Kedah State Association [2015-18].

Peter Chew also is CEO PCET, Ventures, Malaysia, PCET is a long research associate of IMRF (International Multidisciplinary Research Foundation), Institute of higher Education & Research with its HQ at India and Academic Chapters all over the world, PCET also Conference Partner in CoSMEd2021 by SEAMEO RECSAM.

Peter Chew obtain the Certificate of appreciation from Malaysian Health Minister Datuk Seri Dr. Adam Baba(2021), PSB Singapore. National QC Convention STAR AWARD (2 STAR), IMRF Outstanding Analyst Award 2019 , IMFR Inventor Award 2020 , the Best Presentation Award at the 8th International Conference on Engineering Mathematics and Physics ICEMP 2019 in Ningbo, China and Excellent award (Silver) of the virtual International, Invention, Innovation & Design Competition 2020 (3iDC2020).

Peter Chew as Invited speaker of the iCon-MESSSH'20 [Effective Prevention Strategies to Reduce Speed of COVID-19 , https://youtu.be/uU89i8uO5Qs] and iCon-MESSSH'21 [End of Covid-19 Pandemic and Prevent Impact on the Sustainable Development Goals, https://youtu.be/6pPaZDGdpiE] and LearnT - SMArET with Enhancement of thinking, Technology and life (Entrepreneurial/ survival/work) Skill by SEAMEO RECSAM [Online course game base learning to prevent covid 19, https://youtu.be/z1YHIWrvuwY]

Keynote Speaker of the 8th International Conference on Computer Engineering and Mathematical Sciences (ICCEMS 2019) and the International Conference on Applications of Physics , Chemistry & Engineering Sciences, ICPCE 2020.

Peter Chew is program chair for the 11th International Conference on Engineering Mathematics and Physics France ,2022. For more information, please get it from this link Orcid: https://orcid.org/0000-0002-5935-3041

Anyone who sends proof of purchase of this book to peterchew06@hotmail.com will receive a free gift of the Game Base Learning Prevention COVID-19 Infection app. This app article share as preprint at World Health Organization, Europe PMC , some SSRN Medical Specialist e-journal and Preprint the Lancet. Malaysian Health Minister (2021) Datuk Seri Dr. Adam Baba recommend Game Base Learning to Prevent Infection from COVID-19 to Malaysian to prevent Covid-19 [https://youtu.be/rQWuMxbbPhM] .

Peter Chew

Biochemist, Mathematician and Inventor.

GAME BASE LEARNING TO PREVENT
INFECTION FROM COVID-19

TABLE OF CONTENTS

TABLE OF CONTENTS

TABLE OF CONTENTS

Chapter 1

Game Base Learning to Prevent Infection from COVID-19

Peter Chew

Abstract

Background

The severe acute respiratory syndrome coronavirus 2 (covid-19) spread globally, the World Health Organization wants everyone to stay at home and play video games. In addition, one of the conditions for the World Health Organization to end the coronavirus lockdown is for the community to be fully educated, engaged and empowered to live under a new normal. Therefore, one of the solutions is to create a new game so that everyone (especially students) knows how to prevent COVID-19 infection by playing the game.

Methods

Everyone wearing a mask in public places and testing everyone who has been in contact with COVID-19 patients can reduce COVID-19 infections. Therefore, this new game let everyone know the importance of these two prevention strategies. In the game, if you use the M key (everyone wears a mask in the public place strategy), you can easily win the game.

In addition, you need to find all the silent carriers before you can win the game and enter the next level. The purpose is to let everyone know that in order to prevent any serious infection from the subsequent COVID-19 wave, the country must concentrate on finding all silent carriers like China.

The wrong prevention strategies are responsible for the higher rate of covid-19 infection in the second wave of covid-19 in some countries, where asymptomatic carriers (silent carriers) are not tested and isolated, resulting in accumulation many silent carriers. These silent carriers caused a high degree of infection in these countries in the second wave of covid-19.

The game will show the situation. When the second COVID-19 wave arrives, L4 countries will face many viruses from many silent carriers. In the game, L1 represents China and South Korea, L2 and L3 represent Taiwan, Hong Kong, and L4 represents the United States, Britain, Italy and other countries.

Results

After 50 people finished the game; they knew how to use the M key to easily win the game. When playing games, they know the actual situation, so they know how to easily prevent high infection rates in any country

Conclusions

The main purpose of the game is to educate everyone in countries infected with covid-19 to understand the importance of everyone wearing masks in public places, and must concentrate on finding all silent carriers like China to prevent any serious infection of the subsequent covid19 wave.

Keywords: COVID-19, Game, Biochemist, Global issue analyst

1.1 Background / introduction

In response, the World Health Organization wants everyone to stay at home and play video games. In addition, one of the conditions for the World Health Organization to end the coronavirus lockdown is for the community to be fully educated, engaged and empowered to live under a new normal. Therefore, one of the solutions is to create a new game so that everyone (especially students) knows how to prevent COVID-19 infection by playing the game. **Video clips related to this can be found in this link** https://youtu.be/u9uA7HZGW7w . In addition to wearing masks, the application of other methods is also essential to prevent covid19. Prevention methods can be divided into two types: external prevention and internal prevention.

1.1.1 External prevention

External precautions, such as wearing masks, avoiding crowded places and garbage, petting animals, coughing, sneezing, and remember to wash your hands with soapy water. If it is not necessary, do not go to the hospital, if necessary; do not take the elderly and children.

1.1.2 Internal prevention

Enhance the body's immune system can fight back covid-19, Melbourne researchers have mapped immune responses from one of Australia's first novel coronavirus (COVID-19) patients, showing the body's ability to fight virus covid-19 and **recover from the infection. Published in Nature Medicine** [Irani Thevarajan et all 2020] is a detailed report of how the patient's immune system responded to the virus.

Enhance the body's immune system can through Nutrition and stay Hydrated. An article, Nutrition and Immunity, the Nutrition Source publish at T.H. Harvard TH Chan School of Public Health state during the flu season or times of illness, people often seek special foods or vitamin supplements that are believed to boost immunity.

Stay hydrated: keep immunity up by drinking plenty of water to stave off infection. Staying hydrated helps your body naturally eliminate toxins and other bacteria that may cause illness. Drink plenty of water, especially warm water, which can help us stay hydrated, strengthen our immunity and fight back virus covid-19.

Drink the recommended eight ounces per day, and four to eight ounces per every 15 minutes of activity if you're exercising. In the US, only around 12% of those infected with Covid-19 will require hospitalization, the remaining 88% are people who will manage their illness and recover at home, nutrition and hydration are central to recovery.

A study providing nutritional support for the patient with COVID-19 [Liz Anderson, 2020] concluded that providing nutrition and hydration is an essential part of care.

In a study [Luigia Brugliera et all 2020], Nutritional management of COVID-19 patients in a rehabilitation unit also state adequate hydration must be maintained. Video clips related to this can be found in this link https://youtu.be/rN6LFjSu4w0.

Lack of sunlight can lead to reduced levels of vitamin D and melatonin, both of which require sunlight to produce. Lack of sunlight can damage our immune system, which in turn reduces our ability to resist viruses. Reducing stress, adequate sleep and regular exercise can also strengthen the body's immune system.

The article, Nutrition and Immunity also state During the flu season or times of illness, a balanced diet consisting of a range of vitamins and minerals, combined with healthy lifestyle factors like adequate sleep and exercise and low stress, most effectively primes the body to fight infection and disease.

1.1.3 Wrong prevention strategy

Wrong prevention strategy is the reason why some countries have higher rates of covid-19 infection in second wave. Video clips related to this can be found in this link https://youtu.be/uU89i8uO5Qs. The second wave of Covid19 swept through many countries, such as the United States, but had little impact on certain countries (such as South Korea and China).

The wrong prevention strategy is the main reason why these countries face higher infection rates. Asymptomatic carriers (silent carriers) have not been tested and isolated in these countries, which has led to the accumulation of many asymptomatic carriers in these countries.

These asymptomatic carriers cause high infections in these countries. But China and South Korea tested all people who had contact with covid19 patients, even if they were not sick (silent carriers). Therefore, we call these countries virus prevention countries.

Research teams think that mild or no symptoms might be passing the virus to 60% of all infections. A new study pins down the source of the 'rapid spread' of the coronavirus in China previously— people with little or no symptoms.

The study of Clinical Characteristics of 24 Asymptomatic Infections with COVID-19 Screened among Close Contacts in Nanjing, China [Zhiliang Hu, et al 2020] examines the history of close relationships of diagnosed patients, detects 24 non-symptomatic patients, and reveals that COVID-19 patients do not have symptoms that could potentially provoke others.

The importance of this study is to know that patients with COVID-19 are not symptomatic, highly contagious, the duration of the infection may be 3 to 4 weeks, and that their infected patients may have severe disease.

After Wuhan reported a cluster just six new cases on the weekend of May 9, after 35 days without reporting any new infections in the city. We see that the China city of Wuhan has tested its entire population of 11 million people for COVID-19, The mass testing campaign (11 million people) ended up reporting 206 cases of active COVID-19 infections, all of which were classified as asymptomatic.

The question is, why did the city test everyone if so few people(six new cases) are positive? Because testing 11 million people requires a lot of money and resources. The answer is that China's goal is to identify all asymptomatic patients (silent carriers) in China. In this way, China will not cause any serious infection to the subsequent covid19 wave.

China's top respiratory disease expert Zhong Nanshan said "Right now ... the fatality rate is only 0.9 or 1 per cent," he said. "I suppose we don't have too many asymptomatic patients. If we did, they would be transmitting (the virus) to other people and pushing the number (of confirmed cases).

Zhong Nanshan also said asymptomatic infection is highly contagious. Even where isolation is implemented, the RO value may reach 3 or even 3.5, which means that one person can infect 3 to 3.5 people. This number is very high.

1.1.4 Face Masks

A study, Face Masks Considerably Reduce COVID-19 Cases in Germany: A Synthetic Control Method Approach [Timo Mitze, et al 2020], The city of Jena has seen no new infections for eight days since making masks mandatory.

Since then, Germans face fines of up to $5,000 as wearing a face mask becomes mandatory. The latest report from the University of Maryland [Chris Carroll, 2020] also mentioned that wearing masks in public may help slow the process of the COVID-19 pandemic.

Research reports published in natural medicine [Nancy H. L. Leung, et al 2020], the result identified seasonal human coronaviruses, influenza viruses and rhinoviruses in the exhaled breath and coughs of children and adults with acute respiratory illness. Surgical face masks significantly reduced detection of influenza virus RNA in respiratory droplets and coronavirus RNA in aerosols, with a marginally significant reduction in coronavirus RNA in respiratory droplets.

A research, also shows widespread mask-wearing could prevent Covid-19 second waves. The research, A modelling framework to assess the likely effectiveness of facemasks in combination with 'lock-down' in managing the COVID-19 pandemic [Richard O. J. H. Stutt, et al 2020].

Lead author, Dr Richard Stutt, part of a team that usually models the spread of crop diseases at Cambridge's department of plant sciences, said: "Our analyses support the immediate and universal adoption of face masks by the public. Study also shows 100% face mask use could crush second, third COVID-19 wave. A research,

Face Masks Against COVID-19: An Evidence Review [Jeremy Howard, et al 2020] also recommend that public officials and governments strongly encourage the use of widespread face masks in public, including the use of appropriate regulation.

1.1.5 WHO Sets 6 Conditions For Ending A Coronavirus Lockdown.

WHO Sets 6 Conditions For Ending A Coronavirus Lockdown. Disease transmission is under control, which is a top priority before any country lifts the lockdowns. Non-mandatory masks difficult to prevent the indirect transmission of the covid-19 virus. Therefore, disease transmission is difficult to control.

A study [Jing Cai, et al 2020] data indicated that indirect transmission of the causative virus occurred, perhaps resulting from virus contamination of common objects, virus aerosolization in a confined space, or spread from asymptomatic infected persons.

In mainland China, Hong Kong, Japan, Thailand and Taiwan, the broad assumption is that anyone could be a carrier of the virus, even healthy people (silent carrier). So in the spirit of solidarity, you need to protect others from yourself.

Some of these governments are urging everyone to wear a mask, and in some parts of China you could even be arrested and punished for not wearing one. Therefore, everyone must wear a mask to prevent silent virus covid-19 carriers from infecting others. This is to protect the human rights of others.

As we can see, most countries have adopted many strategy such as cleaning somewhere to become a safe area, but a no Symptoms Virus covid-19 carriers, without mask can change cleaning public place to dangerous public places. We see that countries like the United States try to use mass testing to solve covid-19 problems.

"Ensure that the environment in your country, especially public areas, is free of the virus covid19 before other strategies"

1.1.6 Wearing a mask in public ensures that public environments are not flooded with the covid-19 virus.

Those test negative can become positive virus, after they go to the dangerous public places. Therefore, in order to reduce the persistently high infection rate in your country, the most important strategy is to first ensure that the environment in your country, especially public areas, is free of the virus covid19 before other strategies. To ensure that your country, especially public places, is protected from the virus covid19, everyone must wear a mask.

If those highly infectious countries do not require everyone to wear a mask in public, then silent carriers will flood those countries' environments with viruses. Any strategy will only waste time and money.

This is now happening in the most part of United States, and although some strategies such as social distancing are being used, it most part of United States to be highly infected.

As we have seen, New York has implemented mandatory masks since April 13, and has now reduced new infections of covid-19.

This means that implementing mandatory masks can also help reduce infections in most parts of the United States.

"Wearing a mask can not only protect our self, and also protect the human rights of others"

However, as we have seen, some American citizens still organize anti-mask gatherings or do not follow the mask to wear a gas mask. Therefore, what the United States needs to do now is to educate its citizens on the importance of wearing a mask. Wearing a mask can not only protect our self, and also protect the human rights of others

1.2. Methods

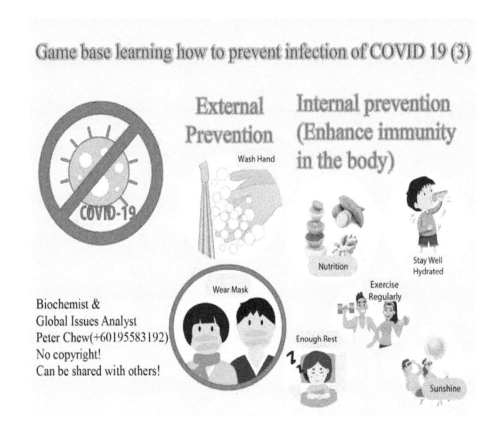

1.2.1 External prevention

In the game, you can press the H key, which means that you are using a "hand washing" strategy to prevent covid19, so the Covid 19 (red) viruses becomes a dead virus (black). In any case, dead virus (black) will become Covid 19 (red) for a short time.

Therefore, if you want to use the "hand washing" strategy to prevent covid19 infect you, you need to do frequent press H key. It tells you that in reality, you need to frequently wash your hands to prevent covid19 infect you in reality.

1.2.2 Internal prevention

In the game, you can press the W key, R key or S key for internal protection, which means that if you press the W key, you will use the " stay Hydrated, drink warm water, " strategy to prevent covid19, so the Covid 19 (red) virus will become a dead virus (black). But the dead virus (black) will also become Covid 19 (red) in a short time.

Therefore, if you want to use the "drink warm water to stay hydrated" strategy to prevent COVID-19 from infecting you, you need to press the W key frequently. It tells you that, in fact, you need to drink warm water frequently to stay hydrated and strengthen your body's immunity to prevent COVID-19 from infecting you.

If you press the S key, exposed to sunlight to increase the content of vitamin D and melatonin and enhance immunity to fight virus covid-19. In addition, in the game, if you encounter a logo that improves immunity, you can move faster. It tells you that, in fact, you need to strengthen immunity to have a healthy body to prevent covid19 from infecting you.

1.2.3 Everyone wears a mask in a public place

Everyone wears a mask in a public place and tests everyone who has been in contact with covid19 patients can reduce covid19 infection. In the game, if you use the M key (everyone wears a mask in a public place strategy), you can easily win the game.

In addition, you need to find all the silent carriers before you can win the game and enter the next level. The purpose is to let everyone know that in order to prevent the subsequent covid19 wave from any serious infection, the country must focus on finding all silent carriers like China.

1.2.4 The second covid19 wave

The game will show how the second covid19 wave happened in different countries, with L1 representing China and South Korea, L2 and L3 representing Taiwan, Hong Kong, L4 representing the United States, United Kingdom, Italy and other countries.

L1 is used in virus prevention countries like China and south korea where there are few silent carries covid 19 like China and South Korea. In the second covid19 wave, their country had almost no problems.

If the player does not want to use the M key (mandatory wear mask) and can find the silent carrier more quickly, they can also win the game. But what is certain is that if you use the M key, although you can't find those silent carriers more quickly, you can easily win the game.

Since L2 and L3 represent the middle-level silent carrier country, there is a moderate silent carrier covid19 in the game. If the player does not want to use the M key and cannot find all silencer carriers faster, they cannot win the game.

It causes those ordinary people to be infected and become new silent carriers, which will make the country a lot of silent carriers and ensure that it is difficult for players to win the game. However, if you use the M key, although you cannot find those silent carriers faster, you can easily win L2 and L3 in the game.

L4 is suitable for symptom prevention countries such as the United States, the United Kingdom and Italy. there are many silent carriers in these countries. Therefore, when the second Covid19 epidemic, we can see many Covid19 viruses spread from silent carriers.

Therefore, for L4, in general, if you do not use the M key, it will be difficult for the player to win the game. If you use the M key, the silent carriers with mask will not be able to spread the virus to the environment. If all citizens wear masks, the existing covid19 virus will not cause any infection.

If the public wash their hands regularly, the covid19 virus will die. Therefore, like Wuhan, continue mandatory all must wear a mask at public area; the infection of covid19 will continue to decrease. What the player needs to do is to continue to find most of the existing silent carrier faster.

After detecting and isolating most silent carriers. Like Wuhan, all activities can return to normal. When the M key is pressed, virus19 will disappear, which means that the existing virus will die because it cannot infect other people who are also wearing masks, and the silent carriers with mask cannot spread the covid19 virus. The environment of your country, no virus covid-19. All you have to do is to continue to find all silent carriers and win the game.

If an ordinary person is encountered, the ordinary person is the same as before you encountered. However, if you meet a silent virus carrier, the silent virus carriers will pay tribute to you. This is because you let them know that they have been infected with the covid19 virus and can start appropriate treatment.

As we all know, usually starting treatment early can prevent patients from becoming serious cases. This is why those silent virus carriers will thank you. It should be reminded that if these ordinary people encounter the virus covid19, they will become silent virus carriers.

In fact, If you test for a negative virus today, after that, if you don't stay at home and you don't wear a mask to go out, you can easily become be infected and become positive for the virus covid19.

In addition, in the game, if you do not press the M key, it means that no one is wearing a mask. When the second wave of covid19 begins, when you approach a silent virus carrier, you are easily infected because the infection of the silent virus carriers is highly contagious.

Chinese expert Zhong Nanshan said that the infection of silent virus carrier's silent virus carriers is highly contagious. Even if isolation is implemented, the RO value may reach 3 or even 3.5, which means that one person can infect 3 to 3.5 people. This number is very high.

As we have seen, most countries have adopted many strategies, such as cleaning a place to become a safe area, but asymptomatic virus carriers without masks can turn clean public places into dangerous public places. We see that countries like the United States are trying to use large-scale testing to solve problems. But those who test negative will become positive viruses in dangerous public places. This is happening in the United States and despite many strategies used, it is still highly infected. In the game, for L4, we will understand the situation.

At the same time, when you find a asymptomatic virus carriers, covid19 may infect more ordinary people and become more new asymptomatic virus carriers. Therefore, the only way is to force everyone in your country to wear a mask to ensure that new infections are reduced. At the same time, you need to find the existing silence carrier as soon as possible to win the game.

" Wear a mask to ensure that new infections are reduced"

Therefore, in order to reduce the persistent high infection rate in your country, the most important strategy is to first ensure that the environment of your country (especially in public areas) is free of covid19 virus, and then take other strategies.

To ensure that your country (especially public places) is protected from the covid19 virus, everyone must wear a mask. If those highly infectious countries do not require everyone to wear masks in public places, then silent carriers will fill the environment of these countries with viruses. Any strategy will only waste time and money.

For L4, we will understand the situation. When the second wave of covid19 is reached, the asymptomatic virus carriers without wearing a mask will spread virus to your country environment. Many normal people will be infected and become new asymptomatic virus carriers, the situation will become worse, if you still do not press the M key, then the game will lag, due to too many viruses.

It shows that the country's health system may be difficult to deal with. Although the method of staying at home is effective, but it will have a major impact on the economy of any country, which is why it is not recommended in this game. The game only recommends effective methods that will not have a major impact on that country's economy.

" **The game only recommends effective methods that will not have a major impact on that country's economy**".

1.2.5 Wrong prevention strategy is the reason why some countries have higher rates of covid-19 infection in second wave.

In the game, you need to find all the silent carriers before you can win the game and enter the next level. The purpose is to let everyone know that to prevent any serious infection of the subsequent covid19 wave, the country must focus find all silent carriers like China.

1.2.6 For countries with non-mandatory masks, disease transmission is difficult to control.

In the game, it shows this situation. If you are meeting with an ordinary person for the first time, this does not mean that he will not be infected by the virus transmitted by the silent virus carrier thereafter, even if the ordinary person is away from the silent virus. Therefore, players need to test the same person multiple times.

Therefore, in practice, this means that countries without mandatory masks in public places must often test the same person, which is difficult to implement in any country. Therefore, if these countries do not have mandatory masks in public places, the Disease transmission in the country is uncontrolled, and the lifting of the lockdowns may lead to new high levels of infection.

A research show that other mitigation measures, such as social distancing implemented in the United States, are insufficient by themselves in protecting the public. Due to the above results, in the game, if you press the D key, the "social distancing" strategy is used to prevent Covid19; the Covid 19 (red) virus will not become a dead virus (black).

Therefore, if you use a "social distancing" strategy to prevent covid19 from infecting you, then it does not actually protect you from infection. In any case, if your country has mandatory everyone wearing a masks at public area plus social distancing strategy, it will be a plus.

1.3 Results

This study provided an overview of after 50 people finished the game; they knew how to use the M key can easily to win the game. As they play the game, they know the real situation, so they know how to easily prevent high infection rates in any country. Those countries that continue to face high infection of covid19 or fear of the next wave of covid19 are because they still do not know which practical method must be used to prevent the spread of covid19. In addition,

After testing 50 people playing the game, no one can pass L4 without using the M key. It shows for those L4 countries such as the US, UK and Italy. If those country not mandatory everyone to wearing a mask, despite some strategies, it is often difficult to reduce the country 's high infection rate during the second covid19 epidemic.

For players who do not use the M key, in L4, they usually encounter many covid19 viruses, and the game is lagging, which indicates that the country's medical system may be difficult to deal with. Like what happened in the United States, many people were infected and died.

1.4. Conclusion

This game is to let everyone know the practical way to solve the widespread spread of covid19 in the country and prevent the next wave of high infection of covid19. A research, 100% face mask use could crush second, third COVID-19 wave.

The research, A modelling framework to assess the likely effectiveness of facemasks in combination with 'lock-down' in managing the COVID-19 pandemic. led by scientists at the Britain's Cambridge and Greenwich Universities, suggests lockdowns alone will not stop the resurgence of the new SARS-CoV-2 coronavirus, but that even homemade masks can dramatically reduce transmission rates if enough people wear them in public.

In the game, if you use the M key, you can easily win the game (everyone wear a mask in public places). In L4, if you do not use the M key, it is difficult to win the game. The purpose is to educate everyone in countries with high covid-19 infection rates to know the importance of everyone wearing a mask in public places.

In the game, you need to find all the silent carriers before you can win the game and enter the next level. The purpose is to let everyone know that to prevent any serious infection of the subsequent covid19 wave, the country must focus find all silent carriers like China.

Funding

The author(s) received no financial support for the research, authorship, and/or publication of this article.

Author Information

Corresponding author: *peterchew999@hotmail.my*

Declaration of conflicting interests.

The author(s) declared no potential conflicts of interest with respect to the research, authorship, and/or publication of this article.

Ethical approval:

This article does not contain any studies with human participants or animals performed by any of the authors.

1.5 References

1.   Irani Thevarajan, Nguyen Thi H. O. N, Marios Koutsakos, Julian Druce, Leon Caly, Sandt Carolien E. van de, Xiaoxiao Jia, Suellen Nicholson, Mike Catton, Cowie Benjamin, Tong Steven Y. C, Lewin Sharon R, Katherine Kedzierska. Breadth of concomitant immune responses prior to patient recovery: a case report of non-severe COVID-19. Nature Medicine volume 26. 2020: 453-455. [Published: 16 March 2020]

2. Liz Anderson. Providing nutritional support for the patient with COVID-19. British Journal of Nursing. 2020 Apr 23; 29(8). Published Online: https://doi.org/10.12968/bjon.2020.29.8.458

3. Luigia Brugliera, Alfio Spina, Paola Castellazzi, Paolo Cimino, Pietro   Arcuri, Alessandra   Negro, Elise Houdayer, Federica Alemanno, Alessandra Giordani, Mortini Pietro, Sandro Iannaccone. Nutritional management of COVID-19 patients in a rehabilitation unit. European Journal of Clinical Nutrition. 2020 May 20; 74: 860-863. Published:

4. Zhiliang Hu, Ci Song, Chuanjun Xu, Guangfu Jin, Yaling Chen, Xin Xu, Hongxia Ma, Wei Chen, Yuan Lin, Yishan Zheng, Jianming Wang, zhibin hu, Yongxiang Y, Hongbing Shen. Clinical Characteristics of 24 Asymptomatic Infections with COVID-19 Screened among Close Contacts in Nanjing. China: Science China Life. Feb 20, 20 https://doi.org/10.1007/s11427-020-1661-4

5. Timo Mitze, Reinhold Kosfeld, Johannes Rode, Klaus Wälde. Face Masks Considerably Reduce COVID-19 Cases in Germany: A Synthetic Control Method Approach. 2020 JUNE.
6. Chris Carroll. University of Maryland. 2020 April 3. Wearing surgical masks in public could help slow COVID-19 pandemic's advance

7. Leung Nancy H L, Chu Daniel K W, Shiu Eunice Y C, Kwok-Hung Chan, McDevitt James J, Hau Benien J P, Hui-Ling Yen, Yuguo Li, Dennis KMI, Peiris J S Malik, Seto Wing-Hong, Leung Gabriel M, Milton Donald K, Cowling Benjamin J. Respiratory virus shedding in exhaled breath and efficacy of face masks. Nature Medicine. 2020. https://doi.org/10.1038/s41591-020-0843-2

8.Stutt Richard O. J. H, Renata Retkute, Michael Bradley, Gilligan Christopher A, John Colvin. A modelling framework to assess the likely effectiveness of facemasks in combination with 'lock-down' in managing the COVID-19 pandemic. 2020 June 10. Published: https://doi.org/10.1098/rspa.2020.0376

9.Jeremy Howard, Austin Huang, hiyuan Li, Zeynep Tufekci, Vladimir Zdimal, Helene-Marivander Westhuizen, Arnevon Delft, Amy Price, Lex Fridman, Lei-Han Tang, Viola Tang, Watson Gregory L, Bax Christina E, Reshama Shaikh, Frederik Questier, Danny Hernandez, Chu Larry F, Ramirez Christina M, Rimoin Anne W. Face Masks Against COVID-19: An Evidence Review. 2020 April 12. Online: (17:41:10 CEST)

10.Cai Jing, Sun Wenjie, Huang Jianping, Gamber Michelle, Huang Jianping, Wu Jing, Guiqing He. Indirect Virus Transmission in Cluster of COVID-19 Cases, Wenzhou, China, 2020. 2020 June 6.

11. Renyi Zhang, View ORCID Profile, Yixin Li, Zhang Annie L, View ORCID Profile, Yuan Wang, Molina Mario J, PNAS. Identifying airborne transmission as the dominant route for the spread of COVID-19. 2020 June 30; 117(26): 14857-14863. first published June 11, 2020 https://doi.org/10.1073/pnas.2009637117

2.App raises public awareness of the importance of Covid-19 vaccination

Peter Chew [1]

Abstract

Background

The World Health Organization wants everyone to stay at home and play video games. In addition, some of the condition for the World Health Organization to end the coronavirus lockdown are the transmission is controlled and the community to be fully educated, engaged and empowered to live under a new normal.

A studies, published in the Lancet, Early rate reductions of SARS-CoV-2 infection and COVID-19 in BNT162b2 vaccine recipients [Sharon Amit et all 2021], find COVID-19 vaccine reduces transmission. Therefore, one of the best solutions is to create an App raises public awareness of the importance of Covid-19 vaccination.

Methods

Vaccination against COVID-19 and following EIP (external and internal prevention) can reduce transmission of covid-19 for the third wave of covid-19. Therefore, this App aims to raises public awareness of the importance of Covid-19 vaccination and following EIP.

In the App, if player press an ordinary person, the sentence of getting vaccinated and follow the EIP will appear for a while, it means that player have been vaccinated the ordinary person and the ordinary person is following the EIP.

Therefore, the ordinary person will not be infected with the covid-19 virus in the future. In addition, player need to find all silent carriers before player can win the existing level and advance to the next level.

According to study [Sharon Amit et al., 2021], the COVID-19 vaccine was found to reduce transmission. For all SARS-CoV-2 positives, after the first dose,, adjusted rate reduction compared with unvaccinated (95% CI) is 75%.

In the App, if players are vaccinated with silence carriers, only one virus will be transmitted, while those silence carriers that have not been vaccinated will transmit 5 viruses, a reduction of 80%.

The purpose is to let everyone know how COVID-19 vaccination can help control and reduce transmission. The App will show the situation, especially in high-infection countries (L4).

Results

After 50 people play the app; they knew how to use, press ordinary person (Vaccination against COVID-19 and following EIP) to easily win each level. When playing games, they know why COVID-19 vaccination can help control and reduce transmission in any country for third wave of covid-19.

Conclusions

The main purpose of the App is to raise public awareness of the importance of Covid-19 vaccination so that everyone (especially students) knows the importance of Covid-19 vaccination. In addition, the App has also raised the public's awareness of the importance of following EIP and must concentrate on finding silent carriers like China to prevent any serious infections from the subsequent COVID-19 wave.

Because vaccination can help control and reduce the spread of any country in the third covid-19 epidemic, it can also help prevent hospitalizations and deaths caused by the coronavirus. Vaccination helps restore the global economy with the lowest risk.

Keywords: COVID-19, Game, Biochemist, Global issue analyst

2.1. Background / introduction

According to the preprint study, Game Base Learning to Prevent Infection from COVID-19[Chew, Peter, 2020]. The second wave of Covid19 swept through many countries, Some countries (such as South Korea, Taiwan and China) just have little influence. The wrong prevention strategy is the main reason why some countries face higher infection rates.

Asymptomatic carriers (silent carriers) have not been tested and isolated in these countries, which has led to the accumulation of many asymptomatic carriers in these countries. These asymptomatic carriers cause high infections in these countries. Video clips related to this can be found in this link https://youtu.be/u9uA7HZGW7w.

After the second wave of covid-19, some highly infectious countries continued to fail to implement important prevention strategies against Covid-19, such as mandatory masks, which led to the rapid spread of Covid-19 worldwide. The World Health Organization wants everyone to stay at home and play video games.

In addition, some of the condition for the World Health Organization to end the coronavirus lockdown are the transmission is controlled and the community to be fully educated, engaged and empowered to live under a new normal.

A studies, published in the Lancet, Early rate reductions of SARS-CoV-2 infection and COVID-19 in BNT162b2 vaccine recipients [Sharon Amit et all 2021], find COVID-19 vaccine reduces transmission. Therefore, one of the best solutions is to create an App raises public awareness of the importance of Covid-19 vaccination.

" Create an App raises public awareness of the importance of Covid-19 vaccination"

2.1.1 Vaccinate effective against Covid-19 and safe

A studies, published in the Lancet, Sputnik V COVID-19 vaccine candidate appears safe and effective [Ian Jones et al, 2021], Vaccine efficacy, based on the numbers of confirmed COVID-19 cases from 21 days after the first dose of vaccine, is reported as 91·6% (95% CI 85·6–95·2), and the suggested lessening of disease severity after one dose is particularly encouraging for current dose-sparing strategies.

A studies, also published in the Lancet, Oxford–AstraZeneca COVID-19 vaccine efficacy [Maria Deloria Knoll et al., 2020]. No COVID-19-related hospital admissions occurred in ChAdOx1 nCoV-19 recipients, whereas ten (two of which were severe) occurred in the control groups.

Vaccine efficacy for the prespecified primary analysis (combining dose groups) against the primary endpoint of COVID-19 occurring more than 14 days after the second dose was 70·4% (95·8% CI 54·8 to 80·6; 30 [0·5%] of 5807 participants in the ChAdOx1 nCoV-19 group *vs* 101 [17%] of 5829 participants in the control group).

A study, published in the New England JOURNAL od MEDICINE, Safety and Efficacy of the BNT162b2 mRNA Covid-19 Vaccine [Fernando P. Polack et al., 2020], a two-dose regimen of BNT162b2 (30 μg per dose, given 21 days apart) was found to be safe and 95% effective against Covid-19.

The vaccine met both primary efficacy end points, with more than a 99.99% probability of a true vaccine efficacy greater than 30%. These results met our prespecified success criteria, which were to establish a probability above 98.6% of true vaccine efficacy being greater than 30%, and greatly exceeded the minimum FDA criteria for authorization.

2.1.2 Mutation does not dramatically undermine the vaccine's protection

A studies, published in Nature Medicine,[Xuping Xie et all, 2021] suggest the variant's key mutation, known as E484K, does not dramatically undermine the vaccine's protection. Study engineered three severe acute respiratory syndrome coronavirus 2 (SARS-CoV-2) viruses containing key spike mutations from the newly emerged United Kingdom (UK) and South African (SA) variants: N501Y from UK and SA; 69/70-deletion + N501Y + D614G from UK; and E484K + N501Y + D614G from SA.

Neutralization geometric mean titers (GMTs) of 20 BTN162b2 vaccine-elicited human sera against the three mutant viruses were 0.81-to 1.46-fold of the GMTs against parental virus, indicating small effects of these mutations on neutralization by sera elicited by two BNT162b2 doses.

2.1.3 Vaccination to reduce symptomatic and asymptomatic transmission

A preprint study, publish at medRxiv, Decreased SARS-CoV-2 viral load following vaccination [Matan Levine-Tiefenbrun et all, 2021], analysing positive SARS-CoV-2 test results following inoculation with the BNT162b2 mRNA vaccine, find that the viral load is reduced 4-fold for infections occurring 12-28 days after the first dose of vaccine. These reduced viral loads hint to lower infectiousness, further contributing to vaccine impact on virus spread.

A studies, published in the Lancet, Transmission of COVID-19 in 282 clusters in Catalonia, Spain: a cohort study [Michael Marks, PhD et all, 2021], interpret the viral load of index cases was a leading driver of SARS-CoV-2 transmission. The higher the viral load, the greater the transmissibility of the virus.

Data analysis in a study by the Israeli Health Ministry and Pfizer Inc found the Pfizer vaccine developed with Germany's BioNTech reduces infection, including in asymptomatic cases, by 89.4% and in symptomatic cases by 93.7%.

A studies, published in the Lancet [Sharon Amit et all 2021], Early rate reductions of SARS-CoV-2 infection and COVID-19 in BNT162b2 vaccine recipients The Lancet medical journal found that among 7,214 hospital staff who received their first dose in January, there was an 85% reduction in symptomatic COVID-19 within 15 to 28 days with an overall reduction of infections, including asymptomatic cases detected by testing, of 75%. Due to Vaccinate can control and reduced transmission, So, Vaccinate can help restoring global economy with lowest risk.

" Vaccinate can control and reduced transmission"

....

2.1.4 Covid-19 vaccination can reduce viral load, reduce transmission, and prevent hospitalization and death

A studies, published in the Nature Communications, SARS-CoV-2 viral load is associated with increased disease severity and mortality [Jesse Fajnzylber, et all, 2020], report that higher levels of SARS-CoV-2 plasma RNA had the strongest relationship with disease severity, key laboratory markers, and mortality.

SARS-CoV-2 plasma viremia is commonly detected in hospitalized individuals but can also be detected in symptomatic non-hospitalized outpatients diagnosed with COVID-19. SARS-CoV-2 viral loads, especially within plasma, are associated with systemic inflammation, disease progression, and increased risk of death. A studies, published in the Asia Paciific Journal of Public Health, High Viral Load and Poor Ventilation: Cause of High Mortality From COVID-19 [Shyam Aggarwal et all, 2020].

2.1.5 Vaccine offers 100% protection against coronavirus hospitalisations and deaths

Johnson & Johnson's one-shot vaccine generated strong protection against Covid-19 in a large, late-stage trial, raising hopes that it can rapidly reshape a stumbling immunisation campaign. In the more than 44,000-person study, the vaccine prevented 66 per cent of moderate to severe cases of Covid-19, according to a company statement on Friday. And it was particularly effective at stopping severe disease, preventing 85 per cent of severe infections and 100 per cent of hospitalisations and deaths.

Vaccine AstraZeneca confirms 100% protection against severe disease, hospitalisation and death in the primary analysis of Phase III trials.
A preprint the Lancet, Single Dose Administration, And The Influence Of The Timing Of The Booster Dose On Immunogenicity and Efficacy Of ChAdOx1 nCoV19(AZD1222) Vaccine [Merryn Voysey, et all 2021]. the study find, 17,177 baseline seronegative trial participants were eligible for inclusion in the efficacy analysis, 8948 in the UK, 6753 in Brazil and 1476 in South Africa, with 619 documented NAAT +ve infections of

which 332 met the primary endpoint of symptomatic infection >14 days post dose 2.

The primary analysis of overall vaccine efficacy >14 days after the second dose including LD/SD and SD/SD groups, based on the prespecified criteria was 66.7% (57.4%, 74.0%). There were no hospitalisations in the ChAdOx1 nCoV-19 group after the initial 21 day exclusion period, and 15 in the control group.

The World Health Organization (WHO) regional director for Europe said he believes the coronavirus outbreak will end in early 2022, reported the *Anadolu Agency*. WHO is currently looking into how it can work with member states to create an e-vaccination and states.

More Airlines sign up for vaccine passports. Airline industry app could open up quarantine-free travel. Airlines ask WHO to Back Quarantine-Free Travel After Vaccines. An international rule vaccination and COVID-19 recover patient travel ("Science-based Immunization Passport Rules") is needed to help restore the global economy with the lowest risk.

2.1.6 Past infection provides 83% protection for five months

Oxford study says Covid reinfection 'highly unlikely' for at least six months. Centers for Disease Control and Prevention says Cases of reinfection with COVID-19 have been reported, but remain rare.

<u>Previous infection reduced the odds of reinfection by at least 90%</u>

A studies, Covid-19: Past infection provides 83% protection for five months but may not stop transmission [Elisabeth Mahase 2021], The researchers calculated that adjusted odds ratio was 0.17 for all reinfections (95% confidence interval 0.13 to 0.24) compared with PCR confirmed primary infections, equating to 83% protection.

The median interval between primary infection and reinfection was over 160 days. When looking at only symptomatic cases supported by positive PCR results, previous infection reduced the odds of reinfection by at least 90% (adjusted odds ratio 0.06 with 95% CI 0.03 to 0.09). The study team stressed that these results give no insight into the effects of vaccines or the new more transmissible variant in the UK, because of the time period analysed.

2.1.7 Vaccination still needs to follow the preventive covid-19 strategy , because

i)The vaccine cannot be fully immunized. It has been found that the current vaccine's immunity against COVID-19 can reach up to 95%. That means that there is still a small chance that you could get infected, so you need to continue to follow preventive covid-19 strategy.

ii)You might be asymptomatic, so you can still spread the COVID-19 virus to others. Vaccines just can reduce asymptomatic transmission.

2.1.8 EIP (External and Internal prevention)

External prevention: External precautions, such as wearing masks, and remember to wash your hands with soapy water. If it is not necessary, do not go to the hospital, if necessary; do not take the elderly and children.

Internal prevention: Enhance the body's immune system can fight back covid-19, Melbourne researchers have mapped immune responses from one of Australia's first novel coronavirus (COVID-19) patients, showing the body's ability to fight virus covid-19 and recover from the infection. Published in

Nature Medicine [Irani Thevarajan et all 2020] is a detailed report of how the patient's immune system responded to the virus. Nutrition and hydration are central to recovery.

A study providing nutritional support for the patient with COVID-19 [Liz Anderson, 2020] concluded that providing nutrition and hydration is an essential part of care.

In a study [Luigia Brugliera et all 2020], Nutritional management of COVID-19 patients in a rehabilitation unit also state adequate hydration must be maintained. Video clips related to this can be found in this link https://youtu.be/rN6LFjSu4w0.

Lack of sunlight can lead to reduced levels of vitamin D and melatonin, both of which require sunlight to produce. Lack of sunlight can damage our immune system, which in turn reduces our ability to resist viruses. Reducing stress, adequate sleep and regular exercise can also strengthen the body's immune system. Video clips related to this can be found in this link. The app can be obtained for free via this link.

2.2. Methods

The App (version 4) is an extension application Game Base Learning to Prevent Infection from COVID-19(version 3) [Chew, Peter, 2020].

2.2.1 External prevention

In the App, player can touch or press the photo "hand washing", which means that player are using a "hand washing" strategy to prevent covid19, so the Covid 19 (red) viruses becomes a dead virus (black). In any case, dead virus (black) will become Covid 19 (red) for a short time.

Therefore, if player want to use the "hand washing" strategy to prevent covid19 infect him, he need to do frequent touch or press the photo "hand washing". It tells you that in reality, you need to frequently wash your hands to prevent covid19 infect you in reality.

For the App (version 3), for the second wave of covid-19 using the "mask strategy", all viruses will disappear, which is very effective. But for the App (version 4), for the third wave of Covid-19 using the "mask strategy" (touch or press to cover the photo), the Covid 19 (red) virus became a dead virus (black).

In any case, if the player does not use the "mask" (leave or release the mask photo), the dead virus (black) will become Covid 19 (red). The effectiveness of the " mask strategy " has decreased.

The reason for this change is that the lockdown strategy of some country is a change from the second wave of covid-19 and the third wave of covid-19. For the second wave of covid-19, certain countries can still stop operate of most companies and providing some funds to these companies, but this has had a huge impact on economic countries.

Regarding the third wave of covid-19, many companies are allowed to operate because some country cannot stop operate of most companies from having a huge impact on economic countries again. As we know, workers can not wear masks when eating.

For the third wave of covid-19, the mask strategy effect is smaller. In any case, vaccination can solve most mask strategy problems. If people have been vaccinated without a mask, they still have 95% ability to prevent infection. These can prevent workers from getting infection while eating. However, to ensure that there is no infection, everyone who has been vaccinated still needs to wear a mask and follow others EIP.

2.2.2 Internal prevention

In the App, player can touch or press the photo "Stay Well hydrated", it mean player use the " stay Hydrated, drink warm water, " strategy to prevent covid19, so the Covid 19 (red) virus will become a dead virus (black). But the dead virus (black) will also become Covid 19 (red) in a short time.

Therefore, if player want to use the "drink warm water to stay hydrated" strategy to prevent infection of COVID-19, player need to touch or press the photo "Stay Well hydrated" frequently. It tells you that, in fact, you need to drink warm water frequently to stay hydrated and strengthen your body's immunity to prevent COVID-19 from infecting you.

The App aims to raise public awareness of the importance of Covid-19 vaccination and following EIP so that everyone (especially students) knows the importance of Covid-19 vaccination and following EIP. Therefore, if player press an ordinary person, the sentence of getting vaccinated and follow the EIP will appear for a while, it means that player have been vaccinated the ordinary person and the ordinary person is following the EIP.

Therefore, the ordinary person will not be infected with the covid-19 virus in the future. If player press every ordinary person (vaccinated and follow the EIP) on each level first, player can win the level more easily.

In addition, player need to find all silent carriers before player can enter the next level. The purpose is to let everyone know that in order to prevent the subsequent covid19 wave from any serious infection, the country must focus on finding all silent carriers like China. The App will show how the third covid19 wave happened in different countries, with L1 representing China, L2 representing Hong Kong and L3 representing Thailand and L4 representing the United States, India and other countries.

L1 is used in countries like China where there are few silent carries covid 19. In the third covid19 wave, their country had almost no problems. If the player does not want to use press every ordinary person(vaccinated and follow the EIP) and can find the silent carrier more quickly, they can also win the level. But what is certain is that if player use press every ordinary person first, although player can't find those silent carriers more quickly, player can easily win the level.

Since L2 and L3 represent the middle-level silent carrier country, there is a moderate silent carrier covid19 in the L2 and L3. If the player does not want press vaccinate every ordinary person and silencer carriers, cannot find all silencer carriers faster, they cannot win the level.

When the third wave of covid19 arrives, the silent carriers will spread many viruses, which will make ordinary people infected and become a new silent carriers, which will make the country a lot of silent carriers and ensure that it is difficult for players to win the level. However, if player use press every ordinary person first, although player can't find those silent carriers more quickly, player can easily win L2 and L3 in the App.

L4 represent for high infection countries, such as the United States. There are many silent carriers in these countries. Therefore, when the third wave of Covid19 arrived, many Covid19 viruses spread from silent carriers. Therefore, for L4, generally, if the player does not touch or press every ordinary person and silent carrier, it will be difficult for the player to win the level. If the player uses it for every ordinary person first, then every ordinary person will not be infected in the future, Players can win levels more easily.

2.2.3 Vaccine silent carriers can reduce viral load.

Vaccine silent carrier compared with unvaccinated silent carrier, vaccine silent carrier makes the silent carrier transmit less virus to the environment. According to preprint study medRxiv, Decreased SARS-CoV-2 viral load following vaccination [Matan Levine-Tiefenbrun et all, 2021] and study published in the Lancet, Early rate reductions of SARS-CoV-2 infection and COVID-19 in BNT162b2 vaccine recipients [Sharon Amit et al., 2021], the COVID-19 vaccine was found to reduce transmission. For all SARS-CoV-2 positives, after the first dose, adjusted rate reduction compared with unvaccinated (95% CI) is 75%.

In this App, if the player vaccinates each silent carriers, each silent carriers will only spread one virus, while those silent carriers that have not been vaccinated will transmit 5 viruses respectively, a reduction of 80%. The purpose is to let everyone know why vaccination can help control and reduce transmission. The app will display this information, especially in highly infectious countries (L4). At level 4, there are 5 silent carriers at the beginning. If the player does not vaccinate the existing 5 silent carriers, when the third covid19 arrives, the 5 silent carriers will spread 25 new viruses. however.

If the player vaccinates the existing 5 silent carriers, when the third covid19 wave comes, these 5 silent carriers will only spread 5 new viruses, thus reducing the L4 virus by 80%, which will enable the player Easily win the L4.

In addition, in the App, if player do not vaccinate silence carrier. When the third wave of covid19 begins, when player approach a silent carriers, player are easily infected because the infection of the silent carriers is highly contagious.

Chinese expert Zhong Nanshan said that the infection of silent carriers is highly contagious. Even if isolation is implemented, the RO value may reach 3 or even 3.5, which means that one person can infect 3 to 3.5 people. This number is very high. But if the player vaccinates the silent carrier, since the vaccine silent carrier will reduce the viral load, when the player approaches the vaccine silent carrier, the player is not susceptible to infection covid-19.

A studies, Higher viral loads in asymptomatic COVID-19 patients might be the invisible part of the iceberg. [Imran Hasanoglu et all,, 2020], this study demonstrates that asymptomatic patients have higher SARSCoV-2 viral loads than symptomatic patients.

The study, Transmission of COVID-19 in 282 clusters in Catalonia, Spain: a cohort study [Michael Marks, PhD et all, 2021] as mention, interpret the viral load of index cases was a leading driver of SARS-CoV-2 transmission. The higher the viral load, the greater the transmissibility of the virus, Therefore, the above research supports Chinese expert Zhong Nan Shang statement that silent carriers are highly contagious.

2.2.4 Past infection provides 83% protection for five months

In this App, it can provide 83% protection within five months due to past infections. If the player does not vaccinate the silent carrier, the silent carrier will be infected again after a period of time. Calculate the incubation period from any level to the third covid-19 (the estimated incubation period of the app is 10 days, which is equivalent to x seconds for different levels, and the incubation period for each level is different).

It is also estimated that 5 months is equal to 150 days, which is equivalent to 15x seconds for each level. For example, for level 1, the incubation period is 10 days, which is equivalent to 25 seconds for level 1.

Therefore, 5 months is equal to 375 seconds or 6 minutes and 15 seconds. Therefore, after 375 seconds at level 1, if an unvaccinated recovery silent carrier encounters a virus, it will be infected again.

In this App, if player encounter ordinary people, the number of silent carriers will not decrease. However, if player encounter silent carriers, the number of silent carriers will decrease by 1. It should be reminded that if the player does not vaccinate ordinary people, when ordinary people encounter the COVID-19 virus, they will become new silent carriers, and the number of silent carriers will increase by 1.

In fact, if you are not vaccinated today and test negative for the virus, then after that, if you are not at home and go out without wearing a mask, then you can easily get infected and test positive for the virus at high infection country..

As we have seen, most countries have adopted many strategies previously, such as cleaning a place to become a safe area, but unvaccinated silent carriers without masks can turn clean public places into dangerous public places cause unvaccinated silent carriers have high virus load.

We see that countries like the United States previously are trying to use large-scale testing to solve covid-19 problems. But those who test negative will become positive viruses in dangerous public places. This is happening in the United States previously and despite many strategies used previously, it is still highly infected.

In the App, for L4, we will understand the situation. At the same time, when you find an unvaccinated silent carriers, covid19 may infect more unvaccinated ordinary people and become more new unvaccinated silent carriers, the number of silence carrier at the level will increase.

Therefore, the simple strategy is to vaccinate everyone (ordinary people and silent carriers) and follow the EIP to ensure that new infections are reduced. At the same time, player need to find the existing silent carrier as soon as possible to win level 4

Therefore, in order to reduce the persistently high infection rate in any country, the most important strategy is to first ensure that the environment in any country (especially in public areas) does not contain the COVID-19 virus, and then adopt other strategies.

To ensure that those high infection country (especially public places) is protected from the COVID-19 virus, everyone must be vaccinated and wear a mask. If those highly infectious countries do not use vaccination strategies and mandatory mask strategies in public places, then unvaccinated silent carriers will fill the environment of these high infection rate countries with viruses. Any strategy will only waste time and money

For L4, we will understand the situation. When the third wave of covid19 is reached, the unvaccinated silent carriers without wearing a mask will spread many virus. Many normal people will be infected and become new unvaccinated silent carriers, the situation will become worse.

Although the 'staying at home' strategy's is effective, but it will have a major impact on the economy of any country, which is why it is not recommended in this App. The App only recommends effective strategy's that will not have a major impact on that country's economy.

For countries unvaccinated and non-mandatory masks, disease transmission is difficult to control. In the App, it shows this situation. If you are encounter with an ordinary person for the first time, this does not mean that he will not be infected by the virus transmitted by the silent carrier thereafter. Even if ordinary people are far away from the silent carrier, infection may occur due to indirect transmission.

Study [Jing Cai, et al 2020] data indicated that indirect transmission of the causative virus occurred, perhaps resulting from virus contamination of common objects, virus aerosolization in a confined space, or spread from asymptomatic infected persons. Therefore, players need to test the same person multiple times.

In fact, this means that high infection countries without vaccination strategies and mandatory masks in public places must often test the same person, which is difficult to implement in any country. Therefore, if these countries do not use vaccination strategies and mandatory masks in public places, the Disease transmission in the country is uncontrolled.

2.3. Results

After 50 people play the app; they knew how to use, press ordinary person (Vaccination against COVID-19 and following EIP) to easily win each level. When playing games, they know why COVID-19 vaccination can help control and reduce transmission in any country for third wave of covid-19.

In fact, we can see that after the United States provided citizens with vaccination and implemented mandatory masks, the number of new daily cases in the United States has dropped sharply.

In addition, the number of new deaths per day in the United States has also fallen sharply, indicating that vaccination strategies and mandatory masks strategies are important.

"Vaccination strategies and mandatory masks strategies are important"

2.4. Conclusion

The main purpose of the App is to raise public awareness of the importance of Covid-19 vaccination so that everyone (especially students) knows the importance of Covid-19 vaccination. In addition, the App has also raised the public's awareness of the importance of following EIP and must concentrate on finding silent carriers like China to prevent any serious infections from the subsequent COVID-19 wave.

Because vaccination can help control and reduce the spread of any country in the third covid-19 epidemic, it can also help prevent hospitalizations and deaths caused by the coronavirus. Vaccination helps restore the global economy with the lowest risk.

However, we also need to prevent the emergence of similar new viruses to prevent the global economic burden and health threats from being more affected. The important thing is that we need to find an effective strategy to solve the above problems if the above problem occur.

The purpose of this App design is to solve the above problems, not just covid-19. For example, if we wear a mask, the mask can stop not only covid-19 droplets, but also any droplets in any virus. Enhancing our human immune system can also make our body resistant to any virus, including covid-19 and any mutant covid19 virus.

By adopting a healthy lifestyle strategy(Internal prevention strategy) to strengthen the human immune system, any country can have healthy citizens, which can reduce the medical expenses of any country such as Malaysia. In addition, if a country has healthy citizens, it will definitely increase the country's productivity.

Therefore, if any country follows the App strategy, then it not only can prevent the infection of covid-19 and the above-mentioned problems, but also reduce medical expenses in any country and increase the country's productivity. It will help any country recover its national economy faster.

76

2.5 Acknowledgments

Special thanks to Malaysian Minister of Health, Datuk Sri Aham Baba for recommending this application (version 3) to raise public awareness and educate the public to prevent Covid 19 infection. Thanks also to SSRN for helping to share this App article (version 3) with the World Health Organization (WHO), European PMC and some medical specialist e journal. Thanks also to the media for reporting on this application (version 3).

Funding

The author(s) received no financial support for the research, authorship, and/or publication of this article.

Author Information

Corresponding author: ym.liamtoh@999wehcretep

Declaration of conflicting interests.

The author(s) declared no potential conflicts of interest with respect to the research, authorship, and/or publication of this article.

Notes

Ethical approval:

This article does not contain any studies with human participants or animals performed by any of the authors.

2.6 References

1.Chew Peter. Game Base Learning to Prevent Infection from COVID-19 (9/19/2020). Preprint the Lancet. . Available at SSRN: https://ssrn.com/abstract=3696618 https://doi.org/10.21 39/ssrn.3696618

2.Mahase Elisabeth. Covid-19: Past infection provides 83% protection for five months but may not stop transmission, study finds. The BMJ BMJ. 2021: 372. Published 14 January 2021 https://doi.org/10.1136/bmj.n124

3.Polack Fernando P M.D., Thomas Stephen J M.D., Kitchin Nicholas M.D., Absalon Judith M.D., Gurtman Alejandra M.D., Lockhart Stephen D.M., Perez John L M.D., Marc Gonzalo Pérez M.D., Moreira Edson D M.D., Zerbini Cristiano M.D., Bailey Ruth B.Sc., Swanson Kena A Ph.D., for the C4591001 Clinical Trial Group*, et al. Safety and Efficacy of the BNT162b2 mRNA ovid-19 Vaccine. The New England JOURNAL od MEDICINE. N Engl J Med. 2020 December 31; 383: 2603-2615. published on

December 10, 2020 at NEJM.org https://doi.org/10.1056/NEJMoa2034577

4. Jones Ian. Polly Roy Sputnik V COVID-19 vaccine candidate appears safe and effective. The Lancet. 2021 Feb 02. https://doi.org/10.1016/S0140-6736(21)00191-4

5. Hasanoglu Imran, Korukluoglu Gulay, Asilturk Dilek, Cosgun Yasemin, Kalem Ayse Kaya, Altas Ayse Basak, Kayaaslan Bircan, Eser Fatma, Kuzucu Esra Akkan, Guner Rahmet. Higher viral loads in asymptomatic COVID-19 patients might be the invisible part of the iceberg. Infection. 2021; 49: 117-126. [Published: 24 November 2020]

6.Thevarajan Irani, Nguyen Thi HON, Koutsakos Marios, Druce Julian, Caly Leon, van de Sandt Carolien E, Jia Xiaoxiao, Nicholson Suellen, Catton Mike, Benjamin Cowie, Tong Steven YC, Lewin Sharon R, Kedzierska Katherine. Breadth of concomitant immune responses prior to patient recovery: a case report of non-severe COVID-19. Nature Medicine. 2020; 26: 453-455. [Published: 16 March 2020]

7. Fajnzylber Jesse, Regan James, Coxen Kendyll, Corry Heather, Wong Colline, Rosenthal Alexandra, Worrall Daniel, Giguel Francoise, Piechocka-Trocha Alicja, Atyeo Caroline, Fischinger Stephanie, Chan Andrew, Flaherty Keith T, Hall Kathryn, Dougan Michael, Ryan Edward T, Gillespie Elizabeth, Chishti Rida, Li Yijia, Jilg Nikolaus, Hanidziar Dusan, Baron Rebecca M, Baden Lindsey, Tsibris Athe M, Armstrong Katrina A, Kuritzkes Daniel R, Alter Galit, Walker Bruce D, Yu Xu, Li Jonathan Z. The Massachusetts Consortium for Readiness, Pathogen SARS-CoV-2 viral load is associated with increased disease severity and mortality. Nature Communications. . [Published: 30 October 2020]

8. Cai Jing, Sun Wenjie, Huang Jianping, Gamber Michelle, Wu Jing, He Guiqing. Indirect Virus Transmission in Cluster of COVID-19 Cases, Wenzhou, China, 2020. 2020 Jun; 26(6): 1343-1345. 10.3201/eid2606.200412
https://doi.org/10.3201/eid2606.200412

9.Anderson Liz. Providing nutritional support for the patient with COVID-19. British Journal of Nursing. 2020 Apr 23; 29(8). https://doi.org/10.12968/bjon.2020.29.8.458

10.Brugliera Luigia, Spina Alfio, Castellazzi Paola, Cimino Paolo, Arcuri Pietro, Negro Alessandra, Houdayer Elise, Alemanno Federica, Giordani Alessandra, Pietro Mortini, Iannaccone Sandro. Nutritional management of COVID-19 patients in a rehabilitation unit. European Journal of Nutrition Clinical. 2020; 74: 860-863.

11.LevineTiefenbrun Matan, Yelin ProfileIdan, Katz Rachel, Herzel Esma, Golan Ziv, Schreiber Licita, Wolf Tamar, Nadler Varda, Ben-Tov Amir, Kuint Jacob, Gazit Sivan, Patalon Tal, Chodick Gabriel, Kishony Roy. Decreased SARS-CoV-2 viral load following vaccination [Matan Levine-Tiefenbrun et all. Preprint, publish at medRxiv. 2021 February. https://doi.org/10.1101/2021.02.06.2 1251283

12.Knoll Maria Deloria, Wonodi Chizoba. Oxford-AstraZeneca COVID-19 vaccine efficacy. The Lancet. 2020 Dec 8. https://doi.org/10.1016/S0140-6736(20)32623-4 .

13.Voysey Merryn, Clemens Sue Ann Costa, Madhi Shabir A, Weckx Lily Yin.

Folegatti Pedro M, Aley Parvinder K, Angus John, Baillie Vicky, Barnabas Shaun L, Bhorat Qasim E, Bibi Sagida, Briner Carmen, Cicconi Paola, Clutterbuck Elizabeth, Collins Andrea M, Cutland Clare, Darton Thomas, Dheda Keertan, Douglas Alexander D, Duncan Christopher JA, Emary Katherine R W, Ewer Katie, Flaxman Amy, Fairlie Lee, Faust Saul N, Feng Shuo, Ferreira Daniela M, Galiza FinnEva, Goodman Anna L, Green Catherine M, Green Christopher A, Greenland Melanie, Hill Catherine, Hill Helen C, Hirsch Ian, Izu Alane, Jenkin Daniel, Kerridge Simon, Koen Anthonet, Kwatra Gaurav, Lazarus Rajeka, Libri Vincenzo, Lillie Patrick J, Marchevsky Natalie G, Mendes Ana Verena Almeida, Milan Eveline P, Minassian Angela M, McGregor Alastair C, Mujadidi Yama Farooq, Nana Anusha, Payadachee Sherman D, Phillips Daniel J, Pittella Ana, Plested Emma, Pollock Katrina

M, Ramasamy Maheshi N, Robinson Hannah, Schwarzbold Alexandre V, Smith Andrew, Song Rinn, Snape Matthew D, Sprinz Eduardo, Sutherland Rebecca K, Thomson Emma C, Torok Mili, Toshner Mark, Turner David P J, Vekemans Johan, Villafana Tonya L, White Thomas, Williams Christopher J, Hill Adrian V S, Lambe Teresa, Gilbert Sarah C, Pollard Andrew. Oxford COVID Vaccine Trial GroupCollapse.... Single Dose Administration, And The Influence Of The Timing Of The Booster Dose On Immunogenicity and Efficacy Of ChAdOx1 nCoV-19 (AZD1222) Vaccine. Preprint the Lancet. 2021 Feb 1. Available at SSRN: https://ssrn.com/abstract=3777268

14. Marks Michael PhD, Millat-Martinez Pere MD, Ouchi Dan MSc, Roberts Chrissy h MD, Alemany Andrea BM, Corbacho-Monné Marc BM, Ubals Maria MD, Tobias Aurelio PhD, Tebé Cristian PhD, Ballana Ester PhD,Prof, Bassat Quique PhD, Baro Bárbara PhD, Vall-Mayans Martí PhD, G-Beiras Camila PhD, Prat Nuria MSc, Ara Jordi PhD, Clotet Bonaventura PhD, Mitjá Oriol PhD. Transmission of COVID-19 in 282 clusters in Catalonia, Spain: a cohort study. The Lancet. 2021 February 02. https://doi.org/10.1016/S1473-3099(20)30985-3

15.Amit Sharon, Regev-Yochay Gili, Afek Arnon, Kreiss Yitshak, Leshem Eyal. Early rate reductions of SARS-CoV-2 infection and COVID-19 in BNT162b2 vaccine recipients. The Lancet. 2021 February 18.
https://doi.org/10.1016/S0140-6736(21)00448-7

16.Aggarwal Shyam MD, Aggarwal Shreyas, Aggarwal Anita MD, Jain Kriti MSc, Minhas Sachin PhD. High Viral Load and Poor Ventilation: Cause of High Mortality From COVID-19. Asia Pacific Journal of Public Health. 2020 July 25. Research Article Find in PubMed. https://doi.org/10.1177/1010539520944725

17.Xie Xuping, Liu Yang, Liu Jianying, Zhang Xianwen, Zou Jing, Fontes-Garfias Camila R, Xia Hongjie, Swanson Kena A, Cutler Mark, Cooper David, Menachery Vineet D, et al. Dormitzer&Pei-Yong Shi Neutralization of SARS-CoV-2 spike 69/70 deletion, E484K and N501Y variants by BNT162b2 vaccine-elicited sera. Nature Medicine. 2021. Published: 08 February 2021.

CPSIA information can be obtained
at www.ICGtesting.com
Printed in the USA
BVHW090052130822
644458BV00014B/1282